# REQUIEM

LLS

## I Salvator mundi

2

# REQUIEM

for SATB unaccompanied

## Herbert Howells

DISTRIBUTED BY
HAL•LEONARD®

Although written in 1936, this work was not released for performance until 1980, for personal reasons. It is the composer's wish that it should be performed unaccompanied, but he has provided a limited organ part for rehearsal, though this may also be used in performance if absolutely necessary. The setting of Psalm 23 may only be sung unaccompanied, and Psalm 121 the organ may be used only where indicated.

The two small textual divergences from the Prayer Book are purely for musical considerations.

Items I, II, III, and VI may be performed separately as anthems or introits.

Thanks are due to Joan Littlejohn of the Royal College of Music for her assistance in identifying and re-assembling the manuscript.

4

NOV290491

## II Psalm 23

# III Requiem aeternam (1)

12

ter - nam do - na_ e - is, Do - mi - ne._

ter - nam do - na_ e - is, Do - mi - ne._

ter - nam do - na_ e - is, Do - mi - ne._

ter - nam do - na e - is, Do - mi - ne._

ne,_ do - na_ e - is, Do - mi - ne._

ne,_ do - na_ e - is, Do - mi - ne._

ne,_ do - na_ e - is, Do - mi - ne._

ne,_ do - na e - is, Do - mi - ne._

35

# IV Psalm 121

With some freedom of rhythm ♩ = 72

BARITONE SOLO

*mf*

I will lift up mine eyes un-to the hills: from whence com-eth my

help. _____ My help com-eth ev-en from the Lord:

FULL — My help com-eth ev-en from the Lord: _____ who hath made heav'n and

FULL — My help com-eth ev-en from the Lord: _____ who hath made heav'n and

FULL — My help com-eth ev-en from the Lord: _____ who hath made heav'n and

16

NOV290491

**rall.** *dim.*

Lord shall pre-serve thy go-ing out, __ and thy com-ing in: __ from this time forth and for ev-er-more. __

Lord shall pre-serve thy go-ing out, __ and thy com - ing in: from this time forth and for ev - er -

Lord shall pre-serve thy go - ing out, and thy com - ing in: from this time forth and for ev - er -

Lord shall pre-serve thy go - ing out, and thy com - ing in: from this time forth and for ev - er -

**rall.** *dim.*

20

TENOR SOLO *p*

I will lift up mine eyes un - to the hills: from whence com-eth my help.

*p* > *ppp*

more.

more.

more.

*p* > *ppp*

22

## V  Requiem aeternam (2)

# VI  I heard a voice from heaven

**BARITONE SOLO**

For \_\_\_ they rest from their la - bours.

(SEMICHORUS)

S I, II — from their la - bours, they rest from their

from their la - bours, they rest from their

from their la - bours, they rest from their

B I, II — from their la - bours, they rest from their

45

Ev - en so saith the Spi-rit; they rest \_ from their la - bours.

(FULL)
la - bours. Ev-en so saith the Spi - ri(t); \_\_\_ they rest. \_\_\_

la - bours. Ev-en so saith the Spi - ri(t); \_\_\_ they rest. \_\_\_
la - bours.

la - bours. Ev-en so saith the Spi - ri(t); \_\_\_ they rest from their la - bours. \_\_

la - bours. Ev-en so saith the Spi - ri(t); \_\_\_ they rest from their la - bours. \_\_

52

\* omit sounding 't' to prevent 'spit' of consonants

ISBN-13: 978-0-85360-694-9

Distributed By
HAL LEONARD

Scan for
pricing
& details

HL14027133

NOV290491